PICTURE THE WORLD OF
SHIPS AND BOATS

AWARD PUBLICATIONS LIMITED

Holidays afloat

There are not many ships now that carry passengers on long voyages from one place to another. It is quicker and cheaper to travel by air. Nowadays, the big passenger ships are cruise liners, floating hotels that take holiday makers to exciting destinations in great luxury. These ships are always on the move, cruising for most of the year, with passengers leaving and new ones joining each week.

Driven by the wind

Yachts are sailing boats that are driven by the force of the wind blowing into their sails. They are made in a variety of sizes, from small one-person pleasure craft to large ocean-going racers requiring a crew of eight or more.
No matter what their size, yachts can sail in any direction, except directly against the wind.
Many yachts nowadays have engines for use when there is no wind.

A floating airfield

An aircraft-carrier is a warship designed so that aircraft can take off from it and land on it. Aircraft-carriers are also known as 'flat tops' because of their upper, or flight, deck. Below the flight-deck is the main-deck, which is a vast hangar in which aircraft are stored and serviced. Parts of the deck have large lifts which take the planes up and down to the hangars. Carriers are the largest warships in the world. The biggest has a crew of nearly 6000 and a flight-deck covering 1.82 hectares (4½ acres) and is over 341 metres long. The ski jump ramp on this carrier allows the fighters to take off without a long runway.

The tugboat

Tugs are chunky little boats, able to stop, start and turn easily. Their powerful engines enable them to push and pull large ships about, helping them to get in and out of ports, canals or other enclosed areas of water. Sometimes tugs work singly and sometimes two or three tugs work together. Tugboats can also go to the rescue of ships far out at sea, towing them back to the safety of the nearest port.

The supertanker

Oil-tankers are ships specially built to carry a cargo of oil. The largest tankers are so huge that they are called supertankers. A supertanker can be nearly half a kilometre (1504 ft) in length. The ship is so big it would take over a mile to stop if it had to avoid danger. A supertanker cannot get into most ports so the oil is unloaded into smaller tanker barges or offshore storage tanks. The crew eat and sleep at the stern and use bicycles if they need to get to the other end of the ship. Because they are at sea for so long the crew have a games room and a small cinema to use when they are off duty.

Beneath the waves

Submarines can travel on the surface of the sea, but they are really designed for underwater movement. They dive below the surface by forcing air out of big tanks, called ballast tanks, along each side of the hull. The raised structure on the top of a submarine is the conning-tower, which acts as a bridge when it is on the surface. The conning-tower also contains the periscope which can be raised while the submarine hides just below the surface. It allows the captain to see enemy ships without being detected.

The ro-ro ferry

The roll-on, roll-off (ro-ro) ferry has wide, watertight doors at the bow and the stern, through which vehicles can drive (roll) quickly on to the ship when it is loading and off the ship at the destination port. There are parking decks for lorries and cars and above these decks are passenger areas. Large ferries, which travel long distances, are like small liners with sleeping cabins and many entertainment areas. Roll-on, roll-off ferries have small 'wings' on each side below the waterline to stop the ship from rolling while at sea. These are called stabilisers.

Lifeboat

ISBN 0-86163-968-5

Copyright © 1999 Award Publications Limited

First published 1999
Second impression 2002

Published by Award Publications Limited,
27 Longford Street, London NW1 3DZ

Printed in Singapore